YOU NEED MORE SLEEP

ADVICE FROM CATS

Francesco Marciuliano

CHRONICLE BOOKS

SAN FRANCISCO

Library of Congress Cataloging-in-Publication Data is available.

ISBN: 978-1-4521-3891-6

The following images copyright © iStockphoto.com/photographer: podlesnova, 4; LifesizeImages, 8-9; Krylova, 11; michellegibson, 35; wyt-tigress, 36-37; Redzaal, 45; w-ings, 57; Sergeeva, 73; Lulamej, 86-87; lafar, 93; jml5571, 106; molka, 110. The following images copyright © Shutterstock.com/photographer: Bildagentur Zoonar GmbH, 14; Kenneth Benjamin Reed, 19; Mauro Matacchione, 23; kuban_girl, 26; Frank Wasserfuehrer, 31; Filip Miletic, 40; Alena Ozerova, 48; alexytrener, 53; Renata Osinska, 60-61; MaxyM, 65, 89; Lars Christensen, 68-69; George Spade, 76; Vitaly Titov & Maria Sidelnikova, 80; Borislav Borisov, 96; Africa Studio, 100.

Manufactured in China

Designed by Amanda Sim

10 9 8 7 6 5 4 3 2

Chronicle Books LLC
680 Second Street
San Francisco, California 94107
www.chroniclebooks.com

FRaNK MARCIULIaNO

❀ ❀ ❀

To my childhood cat Bettina, who taught me
everything I know except how to lie on top of
a refrigerator without falling off.

❀ ❀ ❀

Contents

❧   ❧   ❧

Listen to the Cats

❖ ❖ ❖

How many times have you felt overwhelmed by life only to look over and see your cat sprawled out on your coffee table, enjoying hour five of his third nap of the day? How many times have you overanalyzed your every little action only to notice your cat peeing in full view of everyone, sometimes locking eyes with you as if to say, "'Sup?" How many times have you been stymied by indecision only to watch your cat walk straight up to a glass and slap it to the floor because it's Tuesday and things have got to get done?

Yes, for eons cats have led lives of utter confidence, complete independence, and blissful indifference while people continue to drive themselves to the brink of insanity with self-doubt, neediness, and the horrifying sensation that whatever they just texted, tweeted, or emailed will be the very end of their job, relationship, or reputation.

But fear not, fretting human. The cats are here to help. Yes, for the first time in history our feline betters have gathered all their wisdom, philosophy, and unwavering belief that their way is the only way into one life-altering, ego-enhancing guide. Whether it's coping with romance, surviving a social gathering, or clawing your way to the top of the corporate ladder only to realize you can't get down, the cats in this book will show you how to achieve serenity, certainty, and almost preternatural self-involvement, even if you choose not to do any of it while proudly strutting around naked.

So start reading this book and embark on a new chapter in your own life. And maybe next time you see a cat doing his thing you can tell him, "Yes. YES! That's how I should live!" Then knowingly smile as he ignores everything you just said.

CHAPTER I

Personal Relationships

✦ ❀ ✦

For when you sporadically realize
you share a life with someone.

Always Stay at Least 30 Feet from a Loved One

———

A healthy relationship is as much about being together as it is as about personal space. And the best way to accomplish the latter is by never, ever sitting still. If your partner enters the room, get up and leave. If they follow you, make for the stairs. If they pursue, do a hard turn into the bedroom, bank off the dresser, double-back into the hall, careen into the home office, swipe the workstation clean, fall into a wastebasket, and go back down the stairs. Keep running until they go to work and you get the eight hours of peace alone you both need for love to bloom.

———

Show You Care with Homemade Gifts

Nothing says "I love you," without actually having to say those words, like a homemade gift. Your partner will appreciate the thought and time you took in creating it. You'll appreciate that you still have what it takes to bring down a raven. Just make sure the gift is intact. After all, you wouldn't bring half a cake to a party, so why bring something missing its head?

Or if that seems like too much work, you can give your loved one the greatest gift of all—yourself, after you've rolled around in some tape and ribbons they forgot to put away.

Keep Changing When and Where You Like to Be Touched

Like a viral outbreak, a loving relationship needs to keep mutating to survive and thrive. Hence why it's imperative you keep surprising someone with what you suddenly don't like now. Such fickleness gives a partnership that invigorating spark that can only come from recoiling from their touch . . . only to return for kisses and caresses an hour later while they're on the toilet.

Any Lifelong Affection Can Be Summed Up in Six Seconds

Love is never as complicated as humans make it out to be. It's simply about letting your partner shower you with affection for that brief moment between expressing sincere tenderness and trying to instill Stockholm Syndrome. At which point you can choose either to escape or stay put until their legs go dead and their need to pee assumes DEFCON 1 status, highlighting another of life's key lessons: With great love comes great sacrifice.

Smother with Intent, Not Love

Never be excessive in your affections. The more you share your feelings, the more common and valueless they become. Rather, keep such displays infrequent yet purposeful. Press your head against your person's chin, often with surprising force. Lick not just their nose but their nostril to remind them how weird that can be in public. Sit on their face until it clearly turns blue.

In short, do anything that will get them the heck out of bed by 4 A.M., at which time they really should be up making your breakfast or be pronounced legally dead.

❖ ❖ ❖

What's Theirs Is Now Yours

Relationships are about two loving individuals coming together to cram all their things into one tiny studio apartment. That's why it makes perfect sense to assume your partner's belongings are now yours, no matter how well or how high they hide them. After all, the word "share" is jumbled right in the world "relationship." (So is the world "purloin" if you misspell it.)

So run off with their favorite socks. Reach into their beverage for one of their ice cubes, olives, or just to see what 21-year-old Scotch feels like. Play with their every possession, even the ones described as "fine china." The more you treat it all as communal property, the more you don't have to worry about breaking a few things.

Get Involved in Your Partner's Interests RIGHT NOW

Sure, you've never played chess before. But why not jump on the board, move a few pieces, and see how it feels? Sure, you've never had Kobe beef before. But when in Rome and near your partner's plate, why not give it a try? Sure, you've never shaved before. But why not help your partner do it by constantly batting the razor on their face in the right direction?

Share in your partner's interests and the two of you will grow even closer . . . or they will lock you in the bedroom, in which case you should figure out how to play solitaire on their iPad.

Say "Hi" to Your Partner's Friends Once

That doesn't mean once every time they visit. That means once, as you walk into the room where they're all sitting . . . and then keep walking until you've walked out the other side.

That is, unless the room only has one point of entry. In which case you'll have to walk back, preferably behind or under furniture or while hugging the wall, eyes always averted. And if anyone calls out your name, either remain perfectly still for upwards of an hour or make a fast break for it with a total disregard for what you just knocked over or got entangled in.

Look Upon Your Loved One as if You Remember Their Name

Does your partner often look at you, then stare at you, then start making fake coughing noises toward you, until you finally turn your head to look out the window instead? That's because people in a relationship like to be acknowledged. So every so often, look upon them adoringly with a passing glance as you peer out from behind a curtain while evading their grasp. It will make them feel special and maybe even make them look at something else for a change.

Trust the Person Who Feeds You Regularly

Some people lie. Some people disappoint. And some people are so dumb they make the Three Stooges look like the architects of the Manhattan Project by comparison. But anyone who wakes up every day to make sure you are properly fed is the very person you can trust with all your heart.

Unless they go to the bathroom first. Or make their own breakfast first. Or suddenly switch food brands on you. Or try to hide a pill in your breakfast. Or place your water too close to your food. Or don't let you eat someone else's food when you're done with yours. Then it's like you're all alone in this world.

Three Rules to a Long, Loving Relationship

1. Almost never remind your partner that you're in a relationship.

2. Let them mistake your joy over passing gas for a smile of affection.

3. Lovingly hug them when they're asleep so they can't make some big deal about it.

❧   ❧   ❧

Take a Trip Together by Leaving First

Do you spend too many of your weekends snuggled up on the couch with your loved one? Take a holiday from the usual by suddenly departing unnoticed. After a few hours your partner will realize you're missing and commence a frantic search. And that's when an exciting trip begins as they explore sights they rarely ever visit—like crawl spaces and underneath patios—looking for you.

Return just as suddenly by nightfall or the following morning and listen as they recount tales of wandering wild-eyed on all fours trying to find you. Then smile warmly, relishing the great memories you made together.

Never Let Anyone Dress You

Everyone thinks they have excellent taste in fashion. And no one appreciates full on nudity these days. But your appearance is your statement alone, so don't let anyone decide otherwise. Keep bobbing your head so your partner can't apply a sweater, birthday hat, or—God help you—reindeer antlers. Immediately remove any clothes by flailing your limbs while scrambling in a tight circle, as if 100 percent cotton burns. Give your person a look as if to say that loud sound they just heard was your soul shattering.

Make a stand, make a scene, and make like you're more than willing to bite, and you will always be free to be yourself.

Allow No More Than Two Nicknames

Nicknames are terms of endearment (with the exception of those that end in "-head," "-hole," or "-bag"). But it's wise to limit them to two, tops. The more nicknames a loved one gives you, the more you have to remember, and the increasingly bizarre or outright bewildering they become. Until one day you're responding to something like "Boozawazzawoozawoo" in public, forcing you to leave years of carefully cultivated dignity and hard-earned respect on the floor like so many hacked-up toiletries.

Savor the Silent Treatment

Being in a relationship means being in danger of having a conversation at any moment, whether you're trying to have dinner, stare blankly out a window, or hide in the garage. But sometimes all chatter stops because of a disagreement that you have no knowledge of because you weren't paying attention. And that's when you should make the most of the silence. Gather your thoughts. Recharge your batteries. Focus on you. And wake up every few hours to see if they've stormed off the couch in a huff yet, allowing you to stretch out even more.

Show Appreciation so Your Partner Keeps Giving You Stuff

There is a word we cats have when we want to say "Thank you," but we all forgot what it is. Still, it's important to show some nod of appreciation when your partner does something special for you, like get you a toy. Or, even better, two toys (even if one of them is actually an inhaler they bought for themselves). Otherwise, your person will stop getting you anything at all, leaving you with nothing to do but desperately convince yourself that the game "Bat Around the Recently Discarded Bandage" has all the continental elegance of high-stakes baccarat.

Manage Emotionally Needy People

Certain individuals require constant attention, even if you just walked by them in the last few hours. And such selfish demands on your time and your ability to withhold digging into their wrist can be exhausting.

So take longer the next time they call you, waiting until their voice gives out or they notice you fell asleep. Be unavailable by wedging yourself behind furniture. Ignore such desperate entreaties as "But I pay for all your food and medicine." The more you remove yourself, the more they'll realize such emotional vampirism is what a dog is for.

❖ ❖ ❖

Personal Space Means Your Space, Not Theirs

The closed door. The locked bathroom. The drawn shower curtain. Why would people you spend every day with—people who pick their nose or do far worse as if you can't see them a mere three feet away—suddenly want their privacy? Because they're up to something. And it's your right to demand to know what they're hiding until they open the door and you remember you have far better things to do.

Steer the Evening as the Third Wheel

———

Currently not in a relationship? Then make a significant impact on someone else's! When your two friends start to get close, squeeze in between to show you're the spackling paste in their love joint. When they start to get it on, climb on top of them to illustrate how you'll always be there no matter how much they undulate. When they decide to take it to the bedroom, jump on the bed to prove you were naked long before they even thought about taking off their pants.

Always be there for them and they'll know there is nothing they can ever, EVER do to lose you.

———

CHAPTER II

Social Interaction

❖ 🐾 🐾

For when you wake up to find a
bunch of people in your house.

Don't Be Nice to Unpleasant People

Occasionally you will find yourself in the company of a most horrid individual, often in the form of an unwanted guest or other people's children. And occasionally that person needs to know just how horrid they truly are. So stiffen your posture to express disdain. Widen your eyes to convey contempt. Oscillate the volume and frequency of your hisses in accordance to the person's physical distance from you, resulting in something like a theremin powered entirely by bitchiness.

In short, do anything and everything you can that might recall Maggie Smith realizing she's just been seated next to a footman on "Downton Abbey."

🐾 🐾 🐾

Keep the Number of Friends You Have to a Number Between "One" and "Zero"

The more friends you have the more things you have to remember. Like their names. And why they keep calling you. And all the ways you can you get out of social engagements with them. And where you can hide until they leave you alone for good.

That's why you should have only "half friends," or associates. Associates don't expect to see you very often. Associates rarely ever call. In fact, associates are happy if maybe you just pay your respects at their funeral, most likely via video chat.

You Can't Have Privacy

There was a time when humiliation was a private family affair to be brought up at Thanksgiving in front of guests. But thanks to social media, every indiscretion can be viewed everyday by millions under such titles as "Ass Stuck in Shoebox."

That means you must behave as if all eyes are on you at all times. Don't fall asleep in a manner best described as "simply precious" or "somehow on a towel rack." Don't perform actions not usually associated with you, like suddenly playing the piano or falling headfirst into a toilet. Don't move your mouth in any way that allows someone to add a voice track. The more you're on guard, the less likely you'll become a meme.

Make People Come to You

Making new friends is as much about screening out the losers as saying, "Hello." That's why you should let people earn your potential companionship by nervously approaching you while you look at them with an expression that simultaneously says, "Do you have any catnip?" and, "I'll simply go back to sleep if you accidentally fall through that open door down the basement stairs." When they finally do reach you and offer their hand in friendship, stare at it. If they're still holding out their hand ten minutes later, you can relax and they can sit down to start praising you.

Enter a Room Like You Own It and Everyone Inside It

Don't talk to anyone. Don't look at anyone. Do go straight to the food table and shove your head so deep into the casserole people will think you're spelunking for elbow macaroni. Don't reemerge until you have clearly demonstrated that everything there is yours for the taking or they bring out some sort of meat dish.

Dismiss Everyone Equally

If you divide your world into friends and best friends, then you'll have some people who feel a little hurt and other people who feel a little too comfortable asking you for favors like, "Get off me."

However, if you view everyone as beneath you equally—and make sure that view is from several miles above with an indifferent gaze—not only will you be applauded for your fairness and egalitarian outlook, but you will also instill a very clear pecking order that even the biggest idiots (which you now see is everybody) can easily understand.

Steady Eye Contact Is All the Listening You'll Ever Have to Do

Do you get annoyed when people talk? Especially about themselves and not enough about when's food? Fortunately, most people don't expect you to say anything in return. They just want to know they're being heard by someone who isn't their mother. That way they're not being constantly interrupted by "I told you so."

So whenever someone opens up to you, look them right in the eye, climb right on their chest, and nod every two minutes or so. Then go to the kitchen because really, you deserve food or a drink more than ever now.

Keep Sizing People Up

People are a mercurial lot. One day they couldn't be happier to see you. The next day they're screaming at you while surrounded by the shredded remains of something they keep calling "My birth certificate! My only birth certificate!"

In other words, you never know where you may stand with anyone. Therefore it's wise to keep a big distance but a close watch on others at all times, throwing off any suspicion of judgment with an expression of utter boredom that indicates you might yawn should they suddenly burst into flames. After all, even the calmest, happiest person today may be the very one sobbing over six shattered antique vases saying, "It's like you hate me!" tomorrow.

Be Adorable

Adorable is inviting. Adorable is magnetic. Adorable wins people over. Adorable gets everyone on your side. Adorable makes it impossible for anyone to ever be mad at you when they go fix you a bowl of tuna, only for you to gnaw happily on the porterhouse they thought they were going to have for dinner. Be adorable and be in charge.

Don't Let Anyone Talk for You

You have learned opinions. You have deeply held convictions. But what you don't have is a voice that sounds like a cartoon character with two neurons in a slipknot for a brain. Yet if you don't speak your mind someone else will speak it for you, often in that exact tone. Then others will actually believe you regularly say such things as "Nom nom nom," "Me wuv hugs," and "I haz accidentally taken a toilet bath again."

You're Not Missing Much

Worried that everyone is having a better time than you? Stop assuming that you're missing out on some great story and just sleep for 16 hours straight. Then when you wake up at 2 A.M. you'll see that everyone else is lying in bed, doing absolutely nothing, proving once again what every cat already knows—the world in fact does not go on without you.

It's Okay to Be Shy

Do crowds of people make you wish for a sudden worm—or sink—hole to make them all go away? Not everyone can be a social animal. But by continuously alternating between three party locations—the table where there is food, the bathroom where solitude is expected, and the window where you can stare out at something besides the middle distance, your own feet, or the exit—you will look like you're making the rounds when you're really trying to figure out how you got in this tortuous circle in the first place.

Stay Quiet Just Long Enough to Be Taken Seriously

There's an old saying that goes, "Dog, shut the heck up." Because the more dogs keep barking, the more they remove all doubt about their lack of intelligence. But by saying nothing for a brief period of time, by looking so engaged in contemplation that you slide off the windowsill and into an end table, people will assume you're a purposeful, profound individual.

        🐾   🐾   🐾

Befriend People Who Are Good at Things You're Not. Like Opening Cans.

There's a fine line between "friends" and "staff" and a successful individual rides that line all the way to the very end. Surround yourself with people who can do the things you simply can't or won't, whether it's reaching for something on a top shelf or getting you untangled from carpet fiber. Your friends will like the time they get to spend with you. You'll like the fact they keep themselves so busy there's no time for small talk. And everyone wins by making you happy.

Always Try to Fit In

Need to escape an awkward conversation? Find yourself backed into a corner, literally or figuratively? Just fit in! Yes, if you believe in yourself enough you can almost certainly squeeze your entire body into any box, jar, paper towel tube, underwear drawer, or large-size waffle cone, effectively exiting any social gathering. Just make certain to go in head first, since only the most chatty individual will be tempted to talk to your exposed other half.

The Three Rules to Ending Boring Small Talk

1. Walk away in mid-sentence. Their mid-sentence.

2. Lovingly place your hand on their lips after you just went to the bathroom.

3. Keep slapping their nose like it's a piñata and you expect candy to fall out.

If You Must Be Social, Do It at Home

Never hang out at another person's place. Things are never where they should be. The rules are different. You don't even get to make the rules. You have to ask for a drink instead of just shoving your tongue in something. And if you break something you don't hear a resigned sigh but rather a prolonged stream of cursing.

CHAPTER III

Career Advancement

❖ ❖ ❖

For when you want what's yours,
what's theirs, and whatever
everyone is having for lunch.

Network by Stepping on People's Crotches

Networking isn't about making friends. It's about meeting new contacts, making an impression on possible corporate alliances, and quickly leaving before you realize you hate the whole lot of them.

Hence why whenever business people gather you should leap on the sofa, look purposefully and commandingly straight ahead, and carefully make sure to step on each and everyone's genitals before exiting the room without making a sound. People will exclaim, "Who WAS that?!" between short gasps of air, ensuring they all know your name as you stride down the hallway, not certain where you are going except towards bigger and better things.

❀　❀　❀

Maintain a Schedule Inconsistent with Everyone Else's

Anyone who's ever worked in an office can tell you that business isn't about getting work done. It's about attending meetings to discuss how much work needs to get done. And that's a time-suck you can easily avoid by starting your day just as everyone else is going to bed.

Commence work at 1 A.M., making enough noise so that if your coworkers live within a 50-mile radius of the office they'll know you're up to something big. Keep working until about 5 A.M., at which point you should start calling fellow employees to make sure they bring your breakfast. In between, do whatever you feel like, remembering to blame any mess on whichever employee brought their dog to work that one day.

Clear the Desk Every Morning

Inbox. Outbox. To-do list. Pens. Coffee. Phone. Computer. Whatever is made of glass. Start each office day with a clean slate by wiping the workspace clean of any distraction that can be shoved or tilted off the ledge.

This will alert your coworkers that you mean business and that maybe if they paid a little more attention to you then you wouldn't be smacking all that stuff off their desks in the first place.

Stay on the Computer as Long as Possible

Why take a break from work when there is nothing more comforting than your laptop? It keeps you connected. It keeps you busy. It keeps you warm. It keeps making an electronic humming nose that soothes jangled nerves. Its buttons are like back massage beads. The power cord has the consistency of licorice. The little spaces between the keys act like gutters for your drool when you sleep. Plus, the people using it certainly seem to be having fun, so why not check out what this whole Internet thing is about anyway.

Be Happy There Is No "I" in "Team"

Doing things on your own does allow for individual glory. But it also allows you to be the sole target of such scathing criticism as, "But that's your foot in the chardonnay!"

However, if you're part of a team—if you cooperate with others toward a shared goal—then when things go horribly awry you can immediately seek affection or another zip code, leaving your coworkers fully to take the blame despite the fact you're all covered in the same pancake mix.

Don't End Rivalry.
Eliminate Rivals.

At odds with a coworker? Career experts would say that the best way to end office rivalry is to find common ground. But then your rival is still around. So instead make things as unpleasant for your rival as possible. Pounce at them in the hallway. Shove them off their chair. Eat their lunch. Push them out of the bathroom stall so you can use it. Keep claiming territory, keep drawing boundaries, until they learn their place or hide in a different section of the building, coming out only when you nap or leave for a doctor's appointment.

Get Ahead by Getting in People's Faces

In today's world you have to build your own buzz. You have to exclaim "LOOK AT ME" if not in words then in a willingness to jump on coworker's laps or meals. You have to be the focal point of everything, even if someone says, "We can't perform emergency CPR with you sitting on Jim's chest like that."

In other words, you have to get inside people's minds by getting so uncomfortably close to their eyeballs that they say those 13 magic words: "ALL RIGHT! ALL RIGHT! I SEE YOU! WHAT ON EARTH DO YOU WANT?!" Then just sit there stoically as they try to figure it out, because it's not your job to do other people's thinking for them.

Act Like You Don't Understand English

Or frankly any language that's spoken to you. A constant obstacle to communication will free you from all meetings or discussions as the other person ultimately gives up trying to lecture, reprimand, warn, or frantically plead with you. Then they can just shrug as you just settle back into your groove or that cake they bought for some CEO's birthday party or something.

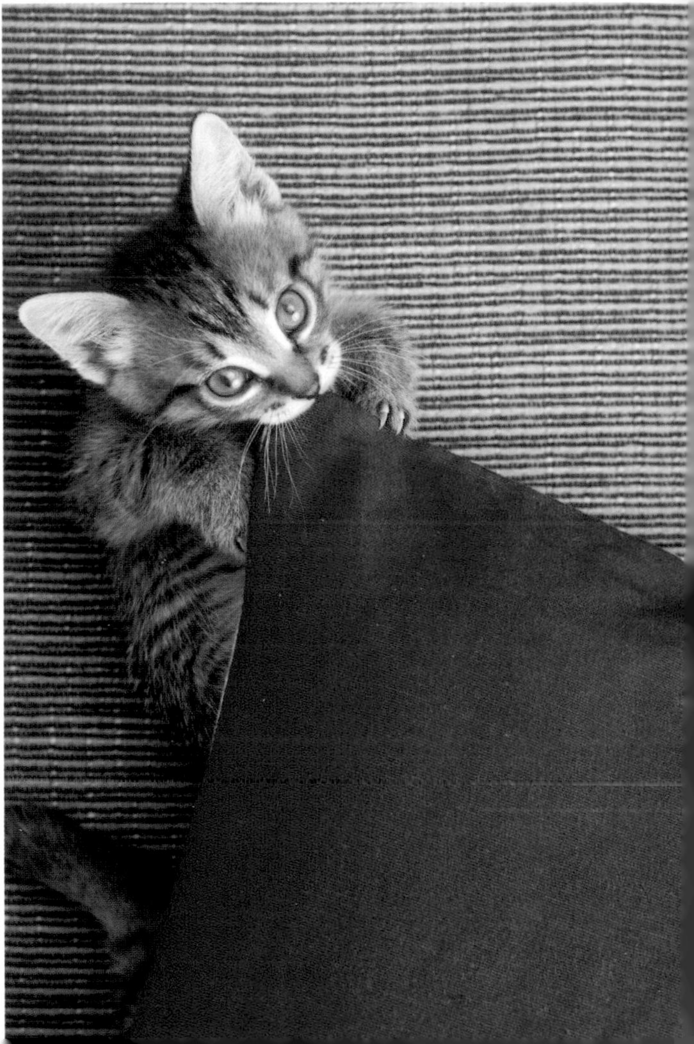

Everything is Prey.
EVERYTHING.

We're not saying you should eat everything (though you should certainly chew on everything at least once, just so no one else will lay claim to it). But we are saying that in life there are only two types of individuals—you and your quarry. Everything is there for you to get a read on, make a break for, and destroy. And if you think that's needlessly harsh or particularly self-serving, always remember—your coworker's feet or that momentarily unattended donut are thinking the exact same thing about you.

Indecision Shows that You're Thinking!

You want to stay in. You want to go out. You want to stay in. You want to go out. You want to stay in. You want to put your foot in mayo. You can entertain numerous, often conflicting ideas at the same time because you're a thinker. You're an intellectual. And you know the longer you take your time deciding, the longer everything remains a possibility.

❖   ❖   ❖

Find a Favorite Hiding Place

The business world—like any world humans inhabit—can be a demanding and emotionally draining place. People keep calling your name, expecting your presence, asking you to climb down from somewhere. It's almost as if they expect you to reciprocate with something more than wide-eyed horror at being woken up during daylight hours.

But the workday will go a lot smoother if you just find someplace to hide for an hour or three. Your hiding spot doesn't need to be far away or even entirely obscure your body. It just needs to be effective enough that coworkers know extracting you from it will entail a great deal of your screaming and their blood loss.

The Three Rules to Professional Success

---

1. Claim every possible seat so no one else can attend the meeting, even if it means constantly running back and forth across an eight-piece sectional.

2. Prevent the company from bringing on new members by constantly reminding them what heck could be if there were two of you.

3. Greatly increase your output by eating things high in fiber, like cardboard.

Show Up to Work Naked

Frustrated by business attire? That's because a tie is a lot like a collar. It denotes that someone owns you and that maybe they think you have fleas or ticks. In fact, any article of clothing is demeaning, whether done for a holiday card photo or corporate ID.

But if you enter the office completely naked you'll be making a statement that you're your own person, that you're completely comfortable in your own skin and hair, and that whatever you sit on is yours to keep.

Don't Beg. Insist.

Never plead, implore, or ask. That puts all the power with the other person, allowing them to demand something in return, like an indication of gratitude. And who wants to enter that infernal nightmare of a barter system?

Instead, always dictate, claim, or press down gradually harder on a sensitive part of the body. You get what you want. They get the message about who's really in charge despite title, seniority, or hours actually awake at work. And balance is once more restored in that it's entirely in your favor.

Withstand Criticism by Not Listening to What Anyone Is Talking About

Sooner or later you will be called into your manager's office and reprimanded for your lack of performance. But rather than cower or crumble, turn your head and gaze at your accuser. Well, not so much at them as past them, perhaps while quietly wondering, "What is that on the far wall? Is that a fly? . . . No, a fly wouldn't be so round . . . Seems more like a smudge . . . Yes, a smudge . . . Wait, why do I keep hearing words? . . . It's like someone is just droning on and on and . . . Oh! It's you. Huh . . . Really wish that had been a fly."

Be a Closer

Nothing beats that feeling of pride when you see a project through, survey all you have done, and say with tremendous self-satisfaction, "Now I know that the toilet paper roll in the employee bathroom did indeed have 1,000 sheets."

Invest Heavily in String

There is no more fascinating product with more uses than string. It ties up packages. It helps kites go up but stops them from leaving. And it plays a crucial role in such classic office party games as "Oh, Boy! String!" "The String Is on My Head, Isn't It?" "I Seem to Have Ensnared Myself in the String," "It's MY String! Let Go!" and "I Unraveled Your Sweater so I Could Make More String."

Keep Learning Whenever Awake

Feeling a little lost in the business world? Then whenever you're not curled up on your desk, adorably kicking a leg in your sleep, explore your office, preferably from shelf-high so you can get the big picture.

Touch everything. Stare at everyone from behind the copier. Keep asking questions, not only such practical ones as, "How far will this bend?" or, "Is it also a scratching post?" but also such philosophical ones as, "How did I get here?"

And if your question echoes, then the answer is, "Because you somehow shoved your head inside a water cooler container."

🐾 🐾 🐾

Scent Mark the Office You Want

There may be some shocked gasps. There may be frantic calls for security. There may be questions about why you're directly aiming at your boss's photos of himself and his or her family. But you're in mid-spray so there's no stopping now.

And why should you? An open door is like an open invitation for succession. And in this highly competitive business world you have to claim your territory, take what you want, and then calmly zip up before heading out for your next target.

CHAPTER IV

You, You, YOU!

❋ ❋ ❋

For when you need to remind yourself to remind others just how incredible you are.

You Need More Sleep

You work hard and you play hard so you deserve more sleep. And if you do neither of those things, then why not fill up all that unused time with even more sleep?

Not only does sleep let you quietly unwind from—or passively avoid—all of life's problems, but when you are asleep people have greater consideration for your personal space. They go out of their way not to disturb you no matter where you lie, even if it means forfeiting use of their own couch, laptop, phone, remote, table, breakfast, lunch, dinner, the sink, toilet, shower, clothes, only clean towel, dog, head, chest, legs, or throat.

So go back to sleep and make the world yours.

———

Wake Up Each Morning As If You Did Absolutely Nothing Wrong the Day Before

If you can get out of bed and walk into a scene of utter destruction that clearly has your prints everywhere on it, if you can look at the very things you dangled from just the prior evening before screws and fastenings gave way, if you can actually climb over someone on their knees, picking up the shattered remains of their once cherished possessions and cheerfully sit expectantly at the table with a beaming smile and a hungry stomach, then yours will be a life without a stress or second guesses.

Make Time to Enjoy Yourself. Thoroughly.

Some days you will run and run and run and run and run and run and run in circles and just stop, never knowing what the hell all that running was about. And you will call those days "weekdays."

And on those hectic days it's important to occasionally stop, take a breath, and whip out your hind limb so you can lick yourself like you're made of ice cream down there. After all, we all have to make our own fun.

Just Because Others Can't See It Doesn't Mean You Shouldn't Chase It

Love. Friendship. Success. Ghost mice. If you can picture it in your head then you should pursue it with all your might, sometimes at speeds achieving sonic booms. Sure, others may exclaim, "There's nothing there!" or, "How many times can you run into a wall and still remember your name?!" But no one ever achieved anything by waiting . . . unless it's to stare up close at a blank wall. Because when that wall finally does do something, oh, man, it's so gonna be worth those three days you sat still without blinking.

Know that Your Ass Is AWESOME

And you have every reason to be proud of it. So show the world! Let people have a good, hard, close look at it, until you hear a muffled reply or, "Great, now I've got hair in my mouth and lipstick on your butt cheeks." Because the better you feel about your body the better you feel about yourself. And the better you feel about yourself the better chance others will agree with a hearty, "Mmpphh! Oh, God, I was in mid-chew!"

Your Best Friend Is Staring Right at You in the Mirror

———

Whenever you feel sad or misunderstood, take a moment to look in the mirror. There you will always find your very best friend staring right back at you. You will also find that your best friend has the exact same taste in furniture as you do. And that they never take their eyes off of you. And that when you reach out to them, they reach out to you. And that in this crazy world you can rest assured you will always have their love and support.

So long as you never leave that spot.

———

Never Doubt Yourself Until It's Too Late

To get anywhere in life you have to take a leap of faith. You have to say, "I can do this!"—preferably in mid-air, well before the facts and all those screams of "STOP!" tell you otherwise. True, you may plummet 19 feet short of your intended 20-foot goal. And yes, you may take an overhead light fixture with you. But as long as you can walk away from any mishap with your head held high and any concern for collateral damage shockingly low, then you will always be a winner.

Ultimatums Are Never the Last Word

When exploring your options in life, never accept "No," "Please no," or "This is why we can't have nice things," as an answer. Rather, wait until the naysayer goes to the bathroom or momentarily shuts their eyes in mid-sneeze, at which point you can triumphantly fulfill your destiny.

The Three Rules to Pure Happiness

1. Love everyone, but secretly, so people keep trying to curry your favor.

2. Take everything as it comes—before someone else can grab it.

3. Never let anyone rub you the wrong way, especially from butt to head.

Never Be Around When Needed

If people can find you then they can ask you a favor. But if people spend all day searching for you only to trip over you as you're sleeping under the hallway runner when they are carrying knives or glasses, then they will think you're secretly trying to kill them and never bother you again.

Be Extremely Independent Until You Need Something

There's a big difference between a needy individual and a highly independent, self-sufficient person in need. And that difference is YOU. You don't want attention. You want sympathy and advice and hugs and someone agreeing that you are going through a tough time right now. That's not being needy. That's being very sensitive to your own feelings, and people should be there for you until you either get over it or get annoyed that they're still trying to kiss your face.

❁ ❁ ❁

Everything You Touch You Improve

You are the architect of your life. Which means you are also its interior decorator. So remake your environment as you see fit, knowing that with every precise slash, every unambiguous smash, every collective shriek as you initiate a chain reaction that single-handedly justifies the need for renter's insurance, you are staking your place in this world.

When Proven Guilty, RUN

Sometimes you will do something so wrong your only option is to flee, since staying put will involve their yelling and your insincere apology. That's when it's best to reflect on your actions from under a bed, behind a fridge, or wedged between sofa cushions, believing you are now indistinguishable from upholstery.

Then after an hour or five return neither contrite nor comprehending of their anger but radiating the message, "All is forgiven." They'll be surprised by your total inability to recognize your own wrongdoing. You'll be surprised to find someone else lives in the house. And it is on this common ground of utter bewilderment that a new relationship can be built.

Learn One Neat Trick

Master one exceptional feat—like urinating in a previously designated spot or actually responding to your own name—and you will forever be showered with praise. You will be rewarded with free food. You will bring joy to others, if that kind of thing matters to you. And if at a bar you will even be allowed to shove your entire head into someone else's Guinness, which can be a follow-up act in itself.

Every Now and Then Be a Little Bad

People are always asking, "What's the meaning of life?" When what they should ask is, "What does it mean to feel alive?" It means getting into a little trouble. It means rebelling in small doses. It means experiencing the giddy sense of liberty that can only come from proclaiming, "It's either me or those tree ornaments and none of those bastards will survive to tell the tale!"

Then don't be seen for three days.

Take a Moment to Wonder Why

Did you hear a noise? Were you expecting food? Were you looking for someone? Were you avoiding someone? Did the house spirit call you again? What so greatly compelled you to suddenly exclaim, "LIVING ROOM! NOW! OW! RAN INTO WALL! OW! RAN INTO ANOTHER WALL! OH, OVER-SHOT LIVING ROOM! OKAY, I'M HERE!!" If you can properly identify the forces that drive you, then you can control your life's path and never look around confusedly thinking, "It couldn't have been for the lamp. I already broke it."

❧ ❧ ❧

Rest Assured Someone Else Will Clean Up after You

Nature abhors a vacuum. Actually, you should abhor a vacuum. They're loud and scary and often have a headlight on them that make it look like you're being chased by the cops. But you'll never need one because whenever you do make a mess—sometimes figuratively but mostly literally—someone will always appear to clean it for you.

Of course, who these people are and why they keep cursing you out will probably forever remain a mystery. But thanks to these strangers who somehow know your name, you'll never have to glance back to see what you've done or how many paper towels it involves, letting you happily forge ahead to find out what happens when salsa tries to fly.

Consider This Your Ninth Life

No one has nine lives. And before you know it you're going to be carried around a lot more than you want. That's why you have to make every day count. So right now, right this very moment, get up off your chair, make a mad dash for the open door, and find out just why the family dog has been going on and on about how great wet grass feels on your butt.

Acknowledgments

❖　❖　❖

This book—and everything I do—would not be possible without the loving support, tremendous encouragement, and minimal eye-rolling of my family, my friends, and all the pets I have been fortunate to call both family and friends.

FRANCESCO MARCIULIANO is the author of the bestselling books *I Could Pee on This*, *I Could Chew on This*, and *I Knead My Mommy*. He writes the internationally syndicated comic strip *Sally Forth* and the webcomic *Medium Large*. He was the head writer for the Emmy Award-winning children's show *SeeMore's Playhouse* and has written for the Onion News Network, Smosh, McSweeney's and the New York International Fringe Festival. He lives in New York City and on Twitter at @fmarciuliano.